You've Got Recipes

A cookbook for a lifetime

Françoise Dudal Kirkman and Jerry Anne Di Vecchio

Order this book online at www.trafford.com/08-0045
or email orders@trafford.com

Most Trafford titles are also available at major online book retailers.

© Copyright 2009 Françoise Dudal Kirkman and Jerry Anne Di Vecchio.
Illustrations and design by Françoise Dudal Kirkman.
All rights reserved. No part of this publication may be reproduced, stored in a retrieval
system, or transmitted, in any form or by any means, electronic, mechanical, photocopying,
recording, or otherwise, without the written prior permission of the authors.

Note for Librarians: A cataloguing record for this book is available from Library
and Archives Canada at www.collectionscanada.ca/amicus/index-e.html

Printed in Victoria, BC, Canada.

ISBN: 978-1-4251-6855-1

*We at Trafford believe that it is the responsibility of us all, as both individuals
and corporations, to make choices that are environmentally and socially sound.
You, in turn, are supporting this responsible conduct each time you purchase a
Trafford book, or make use of our publishing services. To find out how you are
helping, please visit www.trafford.com/responsiblepublishing.html*

*Our mission is to efficiently provide the world's finest, most comprehensive
book publishing service, enabling every author to experience success.
To find out how to publish your book, your way, and have it available
worldwide, visit us online at www.trafford.com/10510*

www.trafford.com

North America & international
toll-free: 1 888 232 4444 (USA & Canada)
phone: 250 383 6864 ♦ fax: 250 383 6804
email: info@trafford.com

The United Kingdom & Europe
phone: +44 (0)1865 487 395 ♦ local rate: 0845 230 9601
facsimile: +44 (0)1865 481 507 ♦ email: info.uk@trafford.com

10 9 8 7 6 5

A special thanks to Myriam Kirkman-Oh
for her creative and technical support.

And with much love to our young chefs and recipe testers:
Clara, Henry, Jack, Tom, Natalia, Alexander,
the twins—Jules and Angèle;
and to our friend, Cleo Raccoon,
who was won back by the wilderness.

TABLE OF CONTENTS

An invitation from the cooks in this book—Cleo, Henry, Sophie, and her brothers and sisters.

If you would like to send us e-mails with questions about cooking, we will be happy to answer. Our address is

cooking@raccoonfriends.com

You've Got Recipes

Françoise Dudal Kirkman Designer and Illustrator
Jerry Anne Di Vecchio Storyteller

Françoise Dudal Kirkman and Jerry Anne Di Vecchio, friends of many years professionally and personally, raised a total of three daughters, who were also friends and playmates. Now our daughters have gifted us with grandchildren, and we have rediscovered the fun and joy of teaching children how to cook, eat well, and savor the social pleasures that a well-set table can bring.

Françoise, French-born and Paris-trained as an artist, lives in Los Altos, California, where for many years she has plied her artistic talents for numerous publications. Jerry, a San Francisco-based writer, spent four decades as food editor for *Sunset* magazine, produced dozens of cookbooks, and wrote many children's cooking stories. She now writes for other publications, too.

Cooking Online

Cleo Raccoon and her brother, Henry, live under the porch of a Victorian house near the Golden Gate Bridge in San Francisco. The lady who lives in the house is a food writer.

These clever young raccoons, who love to eat, have learned lots about cooking because they peek through the window as the writer is making recipes for her books. They also read the food magazines she gets in the mail while they are still in the mailbox. When the lady is away, which is often, they slip into the kitchen to cook for themselves and their woodland friends from nearby Golden Gate Park.

The raccoons use the kitchen computer to go online and chat with their friend Sophie Souris. Sophie is a mouse who lives in a Paris restaurant run by Chef Georges of Avignon. It's near the Louvre and Sophie's family has a private entrance to the museum. Sophie has many younger brothers and sisters. They are all keen to know what California kids like to eat and what else they do.

E-mails flash between Paris and San Francisco, full of recipes (in each other's language) with news of cooking and life in both cities.

From: sophiesouris@jegrignote.fr
To: cleo.henryraccoons@greenhill.com

Bonjour les copains,

Important rules we learned from Chef Georges are 1. Most recipes require measuring cups and spoons. 2. You'll need hot pads when you make hot food. 3. Remember all these basic rules and cautions when you are working in the kitchen.

Sophie and the gang

Basic Rules
Règles de Base

- Wash your hands.
- Wear an apron.
- Read recipe all the way through.
- Set out all tools and ingredients.
- If using the oven, turn it on 30 minutes ahead.
- Measure ingredients exactly; follow recipe steps.
- Use a cutting board for chopping.
- Turn off water when not in use.
- Clean up as you work.
- Remember cautions below.

Caution
Attention

- **Supervision:** Unless your parents say you're old enough to cook alone, have adult supervision.
- **Emergencies:** Call for adult help at once.
- **Cuts:** Knives, graters, and shredders cut. Hold a knife firmly by the handle; don't cut toward yourself. Curl fingers back to hold foods to cut or grate. Don't point with a knife or swing it; carry it with point down.
- **Burns:** Use hot pads or mitts to handle hot pans; hold securely with two hands (or ask an adult to help). Turn off burners and ovens when not in use. Turn pan handles away from stove edge.
- **Steam:** It's hot; be careful when lifting lids.
- **Shocks:** Don't touch electrical appliances with wet hands. Don't run appliances on wet surfaces.
- **Spatters:** Do not put any liquid in hot oil or fat.

Thank you, Sophie, for the tips.

Cleo and Henry

Tools
Ustenciles

Measuring cups and spoons
Tasses et cuillères à mesurer
(needed for most recipes)

Pans with lids
Casseroles avec couvercles

Crêpe pan
Poêle à crêpe

**Frying pans
10 to 12 inches wide**
Poêles à frire

Bowls
Bols

Colander
Passoire

Baking dishes, casseroles
Plats à four

Shallow rimmed pan, baking sheet
Plaques de four

V-shape rack
Grille en forme de V

Quiche pan
Moule à quiche

Cutting board
Planche à découper

Cooling rack
Grille à refroidir

Fine mesh strainer
Passoire fine

Juicer
Presse-citron

Rolling pin
Rouleau à pâtisserie

Kitchen scissors
Ciseaux de cuisine

Can opener
Ouvre-boîte

Garlic press
Presse-ail

Vegetable peeler
Éplucheur à légumes

Flexible scraper
Grattoir

Cooking spoon
Cuillère de cuisine

Slotted spoon
Ecumoir

Whisks
Fouets

Potato masher
Presse-purée

Spatulas (narrow or wide)
Spatules (minces ou larges)

Scrub brush
Brosse à récurer

Pastry brush
Pinceau à pâtisserie

Pastry bag
Poche à douille

Spoon and fork
Cuillère et fourchette

Electric mixer
Batteur électrique

Microwave oven
Four à micro-ondes

Food processor
Robot de cuisine

Blender
Mixer

Timer
Minuterie

Mitts and hot pads
Gants de cuisine

Grater/shredder
Râpe

Serrated knife
Couteau-scie

French knife, paring knife
Couteaux de cuisine

Paper towels
Serviettes en papier

Foil
Papier d'aluminium

How to
Savoir-Faire

Measuring:
Use a knife or spatula to level ingredients across top of cup.

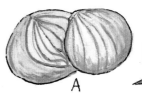

Chopping:
(A) Peel onion and cut in half.
(B) Slice 1 half crosswise.
(C) Cut across first cuts; repeat. (Watch your fingers.)

Chopping fresh herbs:
Place leaves in a glass or cup and snip with scissors.

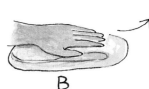

Kneading:
(A) Fold dough in half.
(B) Push dough forward to seal fold.
(C) Turn dough so fold is on the side. Repeat steps.

Sophie likes to visit Jeannot Lapin's garden in le Bois de Boulogne. Indeed, for nibbling, there is nothing like fresh peas and carrots.

Appetizers
Hors-d'oeuvre

Make as many as you want!

Ingredients

Butter lettuce leaves, rinsed
and crisped **

Peanut butter,
creamy or chunky

Tools

Bowl or sink

Paper towels

Plastic food bag

Narrow spatula

Peanut Butter Lettuce Rolls/Rouleaux de Laitue au Beurre de Cacahuètes

Peanut Butter Lettuce Rolls

Rouleaux de Laitue au Beurre de Cacahuètes

Hi Sophie,

Mikey Skunk lives in Golden Gate Park near us. When he is happy, he makes Peter Towhee and us his favorite peanut butter snack. When Mikey is unhappy, he makes a mighty stink and we keep away from him.

Henry

1. For each roll, take a lettuce leaf from the bag**; seal bag and put it back in the refrigerator.

2. Spread some peanut butter down the middle of the leaf (along the rib)—as much as you want. Roll the leaf around the peanut butter and eat.

**Technique

How to rinse and crisp lettuce: Break lettuce leaves from head and put them in a big bowl or sink of cold water. Swish leaves up and down to wash gently. Lift leaves from water, shaking off most of the moisture. Lay leaves on 2 or 3 layers of paper towels (a piece long enough to wrap around all the leaves), then loosely roll towels around lettuce. Put bundle in a big plastic food bag. Seal bag and put in the refrigerator. Leaves are nice and crisp in about 15 minutes but you can leave them in the refrigerator, ready to use for up to 1 week.

From: sophiesouris@jegrignote.fr

Makes 12; 4 to 6 servings

Ingredients

1/2 cup water

1/4 cup (1/8 lb.) butter, cut in chunks

1/4 teaspoon ground nutmeg

1/4 teaspoon pepper

1/2 cup all-purpose flour

2 large eggs

1/2 cup shredded Swiss cheese

Vegetable or olive oil

Tools

Pan, 2 to 3 quarts

Shredder

Cooking spoon

2 spoons

Shallow rimmed pan, 10 by 15 inches

Cheese Puffs

Gougères

Dear Cleo and Henry,

I tell my brothers not to play with their food, but my gougères are so light and crisp, Émile and Jules can't resist a little football. I guess you call it soccer. Thanks for sending Mikey Skunk's specialty. Sophie

1. Put water, butter chunks, nutmeg, and pepper in the pan. Set pan on high heat and stir often until butter is melted and water is boiling.

2. Dump flour into pan all at once. Hold pan handle with a hot pad and stir vigorously with cooking spoon until flour is totally mixed in and the dough forms a ball; this happens very quickly.

3. Take pan off heat; let stand 10 minutes to cool. With cooking spoon, press a hole in dough. Break 1 egg into the hole. Beat vigorously with spoon until egg is thoroughly blended into dough. Add remaining egg and beat to blend well. Add cheese and beat to blend.

4. Rub rimmed pan with oil. With a spoon, scoop a 2-tablespoon-size lump of dough. With the other spoon, push the lump neatly onto the rimmed pan. Repeat to make each dough puff, keeping puffs at least 2 inches apart. To make very round puffs, dip your hands into cool water, shake off most of it, and roll dough between your hands into smooth balls.

5. Set pan on the center rack of a 425° oven. Bake until puffs are well browned and crisp, about 20 minutes.

6. With hot pads, remove pan from oven and pile the cheese puffs into a basket to eat hot or warm.

Tip

If you butter the baking pan, the butter will burn, so use oil.

15

Guacamole/Guacamole

Makes 3 or 4 servings

Ingredients

2 green onions, outer layer peeled off, rinsed

1 firm-ripe avocado* (about 1/2 lb.)

2 tablespoons lime juice**

3 tablespoons chopped fresh cilantro

Salt and pepper

3 cherry tomatoes

About 4 cups tortilla chips

Tools

Paring knife

Cutting board

Spoon

Plate

Potato masher or fork

Sprinkle guacamole with fresh cilantro leaves!

Guacamole

Guacamole

Olé guacamole, Sophie!

This put Henry in the mood for a fiesta. Cleo

PS: *Tip
If an avocado is ready to eat, it feels slightly soft when you hold it in your hand and press gently. If it's soft, it's probably too ripe and will have bruises inside. If the avocado is hard, it's not ripe, so let it stand at room temperature to ripen and check every day to see when it's ready.

1. Trim and discard onion root ends. Thinly slice onions, including 2 to 3 inches of their green tops.

2. Cut avocado in half lengthwise, then in half crosswise. Twist to separate pieces from the pit; discard pit. With a spoon, scoop avocado from skin onto the plate; discard skin.

3. Add onion and lime juice to avocado. With potato masher or fork, mash avocado until lumps are very small. Mix in salt and pepper to season guacamole to taste.

4. Scrape guacamole into a small bowl. Rinse tomatoes, coarsely chop, and sprinkle over guacamole. Scoop guacamole onto chips to eat.

Henry says guacamole is a great topping on hamburgers, baked salmon, even on his mom's crab cakes.

**Technique

To get more juice from a lime, firmly roll the fruit under your hand on a table until the lime feels soft and squishy.

From: sophiesouris@jegrignote.fr

Makes 10; 5 or 10 servings

Ingredients

10 slices crusty French bread
(each about 2 1/2 by 3 in. and
1/2 in. thick)

2 tablespoons olive oil

1 garlic clove, peeled

1 package (5 to 6 oz.) fresh goat
(chèvre) cheese or 2 packages
(3 oz. each) cream cheese

2 tablespoons chopped chives

3 tablespoons crème fraîche or
sour cream

5 thin tomato slices
(2 1/2 to 3 in. wide)

10 thin red bell pepper rings
(2 to 3 in. wide)

Salt and pepper

10 large fresh basil leaves, rinsed
and drained

Tools

Serrated knife

Shallow rimmed pan, 10 by 15
inches

Bowl

Garlic press

Pastry brush or spoon

Fork

Narrow spatula

Farmer's Toast

Tartines Fermières

Bonjour Cleo and Henry,

Start with slices of bread—we call them tartines. If you don't like goat cheese, you can use cream cheese. Do you have goats in San Francisco?

Sophie, from cousin Arthur's farm

1. Lay bread slices side by side in the pan.

2. Pour oil into a small bowl. Squeeze garlic through garlic press into oil, mix. Brush or spoon oil mixture evenly over the tops of the bread slices, using it all.

3. Put goat cheese, chives, and crème fraiche in the same bowl. Mash with a fork to blend well.

4. Put oiled bread about 4 inches below the broiler and broil until lightly toasted, about 1 minute. With hot pads, remove pan from broiler.

5. Top toasted bread equally with the cheese, using all and spreading level to bread rims. On each of 5 toasts, lay 1 tomato slice. On each of the 5 remaining toasts, overlap 2 bell pepper rings. Sprinkle vegetables lightly with salt and pepper. Return pan to broiler until vegetables are warm, about 1 minute.

6. Remove pan from broiler and lay 1 basil leaf onto each tartine piece. Transfer pieces to a platter or plate. Eat warm.

From: cleo.henryraccoons@greenhill.com

Makes 4 servings

Ingredients

4 artichokes, each about 4 inches wide

Water

1 lemon, rinsed and thinly sliced

1 bay leaf, dried or fresh

1/2 teaspoon salt

1/2 teaspoon pepper

Sauce choices

Melted butter

Mayonnaise

Nothing!

Tools

Kitchen scissors

Paring knife

Vegetable peeler

Pan, 4 to 5 quarts, with lid

Slotted spoon

Fork

Spoon

Hello Sophie and company,

Here is a little botanical lecture. An artichoke is a kind of thistle. What you eat is its flower bud. The actual name for the leaves is bracts; the bracts grow on the heart (the base or the bottom). When an artichoke blooms, the bracts open and the fuzzy center (choke) in the heart turns bright purple. Artichokes really grow well on the coast south of San Francisco.

It's very easy to cook them. We love the soft stuff on the leaves, but the heart is the yummiest part.

Your friends,

Cleo and Henry

P.S. We have lots of goats in California, but not in our city.

Good Artichokes
Bons Artichauts

Cleaning

1. Pull off and discard the little leaves at the artichoke's base —usually 1 or 2 layers up from the stem. Snip off stickery leaf tips with scissors. If you see signs of a bug (a brown trail), pull off leaves to see if the critter is still there; cut out the bad spot and discard.

2. Cut off stems flush with artichoke bottoms. With a vegetable peeler trim rough, fibrous edges off bottoms.

3. Push artichokes up and down in cool water to get water between the leaves. Lift out and shake water from artichokes into the sink.

Cooking

4. Pour 2 1/2 to 3 quarts water into pan. Add lemon slices, bay leaf, salt, and pepper. Put lid on pan and set on high heat. When water is boiling, uncover and use the slotted spoon to set artichokes gently into water.

5. Cover pan. When water boils, in about 10 minutes, turn heat down to simmering. Simmer until artichoke bottoms are tender when pierced with a fork, 35 to 45 minutes.

6. Use the slotted spoon to lift artichokes from pan and turn them upside down to drain.

Eating

7. Eat artichokes hot or cold. Pull off leaves, 1 at a time, and dip thick meaty end in sauce, then pull leaves between your teeth to scrape off soft part. When you get to the heart (bottom), pull off and discard the paper-thin leaves. With a spoon, scrape out the fuzzy center; DO NOT EAT. Cut up the heart and eat.

From: sophiesouris@jegrignote.fr

Makes 4 to 6 servings

Ingredients

Vegetables

2 cups cherry tomatoes

4 to 6 celery stalks (pale tender ones inside the bunch)

1 cup broccoli florets

8 or 12 snow peas or sugar snap peas

8 or 12 radishes with tops

8 or 12 baby carrots (3 to 4 in. long) with tops, if available

Rémoulade Dip

1 large egg yolk*

3 tablespoons lemon juice

1 teaspoon Dijon mustard

2 tablespoons chopped shallots

2 tablespoons chopped chives (or green onion tops)

1 tablespoon chopped parsley

1/2 teaspoon dried tarragon

2/3 cup extra-virgin olive oil

1 tablespoon drained capers

Tools

Bowls

Vegetable peeler

Towels

Paring knife

Juicer

Chopping board

Small whisk

Basket

Dear Cleo and Henry,

Making sauce rémoulade takes teamwork. Gustave adds oil while I whisk. Clara and Léon like to watch. The sauce is really just mayonnaise with herbs.

Sophie

*Tip

If you don't want to start the dip with an egg yolk and mix so much, skip yolk and oil, and stir everything else into 2/3 cup mayonnaise.

Vegetables and Rémoulade Dip
Crudités et Sauce Rémoulade

Vegetables

1. Immerse tomatoes, celery stalks, broccoli florets, peas, radishes, and carrots in a big bowl of cool water to rinse well. Pour off water. Fill bowl with more water and rinse vegetables again to be sure they are clean.

2. Pinch off most of the radish leaves, leaving on the prettiest ones.

3. Peel carrots, leaving tops on, and rinse again.

4. Lay vegetables on towels to drain.

Rémoulade Dip

5. While the vegetables partially dry, put egg yolk in 4- to 5-cup bowl. Add lemon juice, mustard, shallots, chives, parsley, and tarragon. Blend with whisk.

6. Add 1 tablespoon oil. Whisk until the mixture doesn't look oily, 2 to 3 seconds. Keep adding oil, 1 tablespoon at time, whisking to blend it in until the mixture starts to look creamy. Then add oil, 2 tablespoons at a time, whisking to blend in each addition until all the oil is used.

7. Stir capers into the dip; scrape into a small bowl. Makes about 1 1/4 cups.

8. Arrange the vegetables in a basket. Dip vegetables in rémoulade and eat.

Nothing cheers more on a cold foggy day by the Bay than a bowl of warm soup, says Henry. Ralph Chipmunk, Angela Gerbil, and Tom Bunny Cottontail agree.

Soups
Soupes

From: sophiesouris@jegrignote.fr

Makes 4 to 6 servings

Ingredients

6 zucchini (about 1 3/4 lb. total)

2 garlic cloves, peeled

3 cups chicken broth

4 wedges (3/4 oz. each) Laughing Cow cheese, unwrapped

Salt and pepper

Tools

Paring knife

Cutting board

Pan, 4 to 5 quarts, with lid

Spoon

Blender

Dish towel

Zucchini Soup with Laughing Cow Cheese

Soupe de Courgettes à la Vache Qui Rit

Salut Cleo and Henry,

Today in the kitchen Azie was singing, "How can a soup so easy be so good?" C'est bien vrai! Find out for yourselves.

Sophie

1. Rinse zucchini; trim off and discard the ends. Cut zucchini in small chunks and put in pan with garlic and 1/2 cup chicken broth.

2. Set pan on high heat and when boiling, cover with a lid, reduce heat, and simmer until zucchini mashes easily when pressed with a spoon, about 15 minutes.

3. Using hot pads, pour zucchini mixture into blender. Add cheese; put lid on blender.

4. Fold a dish towel to make 3 or 4 layers thick. Put towel on blender lid and hold down tightly. Turn blender on at low speed (on high, the lid may pop and hot liquid spurt out). When mixture is whirling, turn speed to high and whirl until zucchini is very smooth.

5. Add 2 cups remaining broth to blender; cover and whirl. If you want a thinner soup, add the remaining 1/2 cup broth. If soup is hot enough to serve, pour into bowls. If not, return to pan and stir often on medium heat until steaming, 3 to 4 minutes. Add salt and pepper to taste.

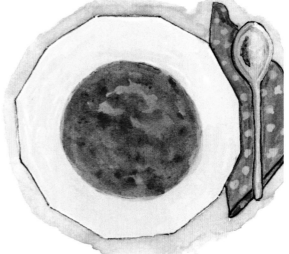

Fresh Clam Chowder/Chaudrée de Praires Fraîches

Makes 4 or 5 servings

Ingredients

Clams

36 to 48 hardshell steamer clams (about 2 1/2 in. wide and about 2 1/2 lb. total)

2 cups chicken broth

Chowder

1 onion (1/2 lb.)

1 1/2 pounds thin-skin potatoes

1 tablespoon butter

1 1/2 cups chicken broth

1/2 cup whipping cream*

Tools

Colander

Pan, 5 to 6 quarts, with lid

Timer

Bowls

Vegetable peeler

Paring knife

Cutting board

Cooking spoon

French knife

Fork

Hey Sophie,

Sometimes we dig the clams, sometimes we buy them. ***Tip**. Use whipping cream in the chowder because it won't curdle when it boils.

Henry

Fresh Clam Chowder

Chaudrée de Praires Fraîches

Clams

1. Put clams in colander in the sink and pour lots of cold water over them to rinse off any sand or mud. Discard clams that won't close.

2. With your hands, put clams in pan. Add 2 cups broth and put lid on pan. Set pan over high heat. When broth boils, turn heat down so liquid simmers gently until clam shells pop open, 10 to 15 minutes.

3. Turn off heat; uncover pan and let stand to cool slightly, 10 to 15 minutes.

4. Put colander in a big bowl. Using hot pads, pour clams with shells and clam juice into colander and let drain.

Chowder

5. While the clams cook and cool, peel and chop onion. Also, rinse and peel potatoes; cut into 1/2-inch cubes. Keep potatoes and onion separate.

6. Rinse the clam-cooking pan, then put onion and butter in it. Set pan over medium-high heat and stir often until onion is faintly browned, about 10 minutes. Add the 1 1/2 cups broth and the potatoes. When broth boils, turn heat down to simmer, put lid on the pan, and set timer for 30 minutes.

7. With your fingers, pull clams out of the shells and put them on a cutting board. Discard shells.

8. Carefully, without shaking up grit in the bottom of the bowl of clam juice, pour clear part of juice into another bowl. Throw away the gritty stuff (maybe 1/4 cup). Pour clear juice into pan with potatoes and cover with lid.

9. While the chowder is cooking, coarsely chop the clams with a knife. Put chopped clams and the cream into the chowder.

10. When the timer goes off, check potatoes. They need to be soft enough to mash with a fork. If not, keep cooking until they will mash. Ladle into bowls.

Makes 4 to 6 servings

Ingredients

3 1/2 to 4 pounds (whole or a piece) butternut, hubbard, kabocha, or red kuri squash, or sugar pumpkin, rinsed

1 onion (1/2 lb.)

4 cups chicken broth

1/2 cup whipping cream

About 1/2 teaspoon salt

About 1/4 teaspoon pepper

2 tablespoons lemon juice

About 1/4 cup chopped chives

About 1/4 cup roasted, salted, shelled sunflower seeds

Tools

Shallow rimmed pan, 10 by 15 inches

Foil

Paring knife

Slotted or other large metal spoon

Cutting board

Blender

Pan, 4 to 5 quarts

Greetings from Paris,

It's amazing! Such a small seed grows into a pumpkin big enough to be a house. Azie chewed out a window and hid inside while Jules did a juggling act on her roof. If I cook it all, we'll have enough soup to eat for days.

Sophie

Pumpkin Soup

Soupe de Potiron

Vegetables

1. Line the rimmed pan with foil, folding up foil edges about 1/2 inch to catch cooking juices. Set whole squash on foil; with a knife poke 3 or 4 holes through the skin. Or lay cut squash cut side down. Set unpeeled onion on foil, too.

2. Bake squash and onion in a 375° oven until vegetables feel soft when pressed (use hot pads), 1 hour to 1 hour and 20 minutes. Remove pan from oven; let vegetables cool at least 20 minutes.

3. Cut whole squash in half and use spoon to scrape out seeds (save pumpkin seeds to toast**). Scrape squash from skin; discard skin. Peel onion and discard peel. Cut onion into big chunks.

Soup

4. In a blender, combine about half the squash, onion, and 1 cup broth. Cover and whirl until very smooth. Pour puréed squash into the 4- to 5-quart pan. Purée remaining squash and onion with 1 more cup broth; pour into pan. Add cream and remaining 2 cups broth.

5. Season soup with salt and pepper to taste. Set soup on high heat and stir often until simmering, about 10 minutes; reduce heat to low and let soup simmer to blend flavors, stirring frequently, about 10 more minutes. Add lemon juice. (If soup is thicker than you want, stir in more chicken broth.)

6. Ladle soup into bowls; sprinkle with chopped chives and sunflower seeds.

**Technique

Toasted Salted Pumpkin Seed Snack. Rinse seeds to remove pulp. Drain seeds and spread in a single layer in a rimmed pan. Sprinkle with salt. Toast in a 250° oven until seeds are slightly crisp to bite and darker in color, 1 1/2 to 2 1/2 hours. Munch warm or cool.

Makes 4 servings

Ingredients

Condiments

2 cups 3/4-inch cubes French bread

1 tablespoon olive oil

1 firm-ripe tomato (about 1/2 lb.)

4 green onions, outer layer peeled off, rinsed

1 cup peeled, chopped cucumber

About 1 cup chopped cooked ham or cooked chicken (optional)

1/2 cup sour cream

2 limes

1 firm-ripe avocado (6 to 8 oz.), page 17

Soup

3 cups cold tomato juice

1 cup cold chicken or beef broth

Salt and pepper

Tools

Shallow rimmed pan, 10 by 15 inches

Wide spatula

8 small bowls

Knives, French and paring

Cutting board

Spoons

Pitcher, 1 to 2 quarts

Hi Sophie,

Today I am making cold gazpacho soup because our pal, Jack Rabbit, likes crisp, crunchy foods. If I add ham or chicken, my soup will be a hearty main dish.

Cheers

Cleo

Gazpacho

Gaspacho

Condiments

As you assemble condiments, put each in a separate bowl and cover airtight with plastic wrap to keep fresh.

1. In rimmed pan, mix bread cubes with olive oil. Bake in a 350° oven, stirring every 3 to 5 minutes with a wide spatula (hold pan with hot pads) until bread is toasted a light golden brown, about 10 minutes. Remove toasted cubes (croutons) from oven, let cool about 10 minutes, then put in a small bowl.

2. Rinse tomato; cut out and discard stem end. Slice tomato, then chop into small pieces; put in a small bowl.

3. Trim and discard onion root ends. Thinly slice onions and most of their green tops; put in a small bowl.

4. Put cucumber, ham, and sour cream each separately in small bowls.

5. Rinse limes, cut in quarters, and put in a small bowl.

6. Cut avocado in half lengthwise and crosswise. Twist to pull pieces off pit; discard pit. Pull off and discard skin. Cut avocado into about 1/2-inch cubes; put in a small bowl. Squeeze juice from a piece of lime over avocado to keep cubes from darkening.

Soup

7. Mix tomato juice and chicken broth in a pitcher.

8. Pour about 1 cup tomato soup into each bowl. Let each person spoon condiments, as desired, into soup. Add salt and pepper to taste.

Today Sophie met Madame Pipelette at the street market. She gossips a lot and embarrasses shy Azie. Émile and Gustave mutter, "She's silly." Sophie hears and whispers, "Be polite."

Salads
Salades

Makes 4 servings

Ingredients

Croutons

2 cups 3/4-inch cubes French bread

1 tablespoon olive oil

Dressing

1 large egg

1 garlic clove, cut in half

2 teaspoons anchovy paste

3 tablespoons lemon juice

3 tablespoons extra-virgin olive oil

Salad

1 romaine lettuce heart (1/4 lb.), rinsed and crisped, page 13

1/2 cup grated or shredded Parmesan cheese

Salt and pepper

Tools

French knife

Shallow rimmed pan, 10 by 15 inches

Wide spatula

Pan, 1 1/2 to 2 quarts

Slotted spoon

Salad bowl

Spoon

Small whisk

Salad fork and spoon

Dear Sophie,

This salad's named for a chef, not for the emperor, and it makes you feel like a king. Croutons are Gregory Quail's favorite part. Caesar Desert Tortoise likes the lettuce.

Henry

Caesar Salad

Salade de César

Croutons

1. In rimmed pan, mix bread cubes with olive oil. Bake in a 350° oven, stirring every 3 to 5 minutes with a wide spatula (hold pan with hot pads), until bread is toasted a light golden brown, about 10 minutes. Remove pan from oven and let toasted cubes (croutons) cool at least 10 minutes.

Dressing

2. In the 1 1/2- to 2-quart pan, bring 2 inches water to boiling on high heat. With a slotted spoon, set egg in water and turn heat to lowest setting. Cook 3 minutes, then lift egg from pan with slotted spoon; discard water. Let egg stand at least 10 minutes to cool.

3. Rub salad bowl with cut sides of garlic; discard garlic or save for something else. Crack egg open over salad bowl and, with a spoon, scoop egg into bowl. Add anchovy paste, lemon juice, and olive oil. With a whisk, break egg into tiny pieces.

Salad

4. Tear lettuce leaves into bite-size pieces (you should have about 8 cups) into the salad bowl.

5. Sprinkle lettuce with the cheese and croutons. Lift and mix with salad fork and spoon to coat leaves with dressing; add salt and pepper to taste and serve.

Green Bean Salad/Salade de Haricots Verts

Makes 4 to 6 servings

Ingredients

1 pound skinny green beans

2 garlic cloves, peeled and pressed or minced

1/2 cup finely chopped shallots

6 tablespoons extra-virgin olive oil

2 tablespoons wine vinegar

2 teaspoons Dijon mustard

1/4 cup finely chopped parsley

8 or 12 whole chives

Salt and pepper

Tools

Paring knife

Pan, 2 to 3 quarts

Garlic press

Colander

Cutting board

French knife

Salad bowl

Green Bean Salad

Salade de Haricots Verts

Hi guys,

Slim, tender, and sweet—perfect green beans for a salad. Skip old beans. They're limp, tough, and stringy. Chill beans fast after cooking, and add dressing just before serving, so they'll stay bright green. Bon appétit.

Sophie

1. With your fingers or knife, break or trim off and discard ends of the beans. Rinse beans in a lot of cool water, then drain.

2. Fill pan about half full of water and set on high heat. When water boils, carefully drop beans into water. When water boils again, reduce heat to keep water bubbling. Cook until beans are tender when pierced with knife tip, 8 to 10 minutes (start checking at 5 minutes because really fresh beans cook fast).

3. Put colander in the sink; using hot pads, quickly pour hot beans into the colander to drain. At once, fill pan with cold water and add beans; stir to cool slightly. Drain beans in colander. Fill pan with cold water, add beans, and repeat these steps until beans are cold.

4. When ready to eat, in salad bowl combine garlic, shallots, oil, vinegar, mustard, and parsley. Stir to mix. Add drained beans; mix well. Spoon bean salad onto plates and garnish with chives. Add salt and pepper to taste.

Quinoa Pig's Tail Salad/Salade de Quinoa-Queue-de-Cochon

Makes about 4 cups; 4 to 6 servings

Ingredients

1 cup quinoa

1 1/2 cups chicken broth

2 carrots (1/4 lb. each)

2 teaspoons grated peeled fresh ginger

1/4 cup rice vinegar

2 tablespoons soy sauce

2 teaspoon sugar

2 or 3 tablespoons chopped fresh mint leaves, cilantro, or parsley (optional)

Tools

Fine-mesh strainer

Pan, 1 1/2 to 2 quarts, with lid

Bowl

Vegetable peeler

Shredder/grater

Cooking spoon

Sophie,

Our good friend, Jack Rabbit, scatters the news about quinoa (keen-wah). Sparrows love this little seed that is Native American, just like Jack. Quinoa is in most grocery stores.

Cleo

Quinoa Pig's Tail Salad

Salade de Quinoa-Queue-de-Cochon

1. Put quinoa in a large strainer and move about under cold running water to rinse well. Drain, then put quinoa in the pan. Add broth.

2. Put pan on high heat; when boiling, turn heat down to simmering and put a lid on the pan. Cook until quinoa is tender to bite and most of the liquid is absorbed, about 15 minutes; stir 2 or 3 times.

3. Pour quinoa into a bowl and let cool at least 10 minutes.

4. While quinoa cools, rinse, peel, and shred carrots. Also grate ginger.

5. Add carrots, ginger, rice vinegar, soy sauce, and sugar to quinoa; mix well. Serve warm, or cover and chill until ready to serve (until next day). Mix when ready to eat. Sprinkle with mint, cilantro, or parsley.

Quinoa is a plant seed that ancient Incas grew for food in their high mountains. Now it is grown, among other places, in Colorado. The seeds (or grains) are tiny and round with a funny little piece (the germ or embryo) that wraps around each seed. When quinoa cooks, the germ turns white and looks like a little curly pig's tail.

From: sophiesouris@jegrignote.fr

Makes 4 servings

Ingredients

4 ripe tomatoes (each 2 3/4 to 3 in. wide)

Salt

1 thin-skin potato (6 oz.), scrubbed

1 cup mixed frozen vegetables
 (peas, corn, carrots, green beans)

2 green onions, outer layer peeled off

2 tablespoons finely chopped parsley

1/3 cup mayonnaise

1 teaspoon Dijon mustard

4 large butter lettuce leaves, rinsed and crisped, page 13

Pepper

Tools

Serrated knife

Spoon or grapefruit knife

Paper towels

Fork

Microwave oven

Pan, 1 1/2 to 2 quarts

Colander

Bowl

Spoon

Salut les copains (Hi friends),

My brother, Colbert, loves to hide in hollowed tomatoes before I stuff them with salad. Today, he jumped up to scare Géraldine Grenouille, but she wasn't very impressed.

Sophie

Tomatoes Stuffed with Vegetable Salad

Tomates Farcies à la Macédoine

1. Rinse tomatoes and dry. With serrated knife, thinly slice off tomato tops. Set tops aside. Use spoon or grapefruit knife to cut centers from tomatoes, taking care not to break through the tomato sides. Save tomato scraps for other uses. Lightly sprinkle salt inside hollowed tomatoes and turn cut side down on towels; let drain about 30 minutes.

2. Meanwhile, pierce potato through skin with a fork in 2 or 3 places. Cook in a microwave oven on high (full power) until potato is soft when pressed (use hot pads), about 5 minutes. Let stand until cool enough to touch, at least 10 minutes.

3. At the same time, bring 1/2 cup water in pan to boiling on high heat. Add frozen vegetables. As soon as water boils, pour vegetables into a colander in the sink. Run cold water over vegetables until they are cool, about 1/2 minute. Drain well.

4. Trim and discard onion root ends. Rinse and thinly slice onions and most of their green tops. Put onions, parsley, mayonnaise, and mustard in a bowl. Mix well. Add cooked vegetables and mix gently.

5. Peel off and discard potato skin; cut potato into 1/4-inch cubes. Add potatoes to cooked vegetables; mix salad gently, adding salt and pepper to taste.

6. Set tomatoes cupped sides up; spoon all the vegetable salad into tomatoes. Serve tomatoes on lettuce leaves. You'll need a knife and fork to eat the salad.

Picnics, Sandwiches
Pique-niques, Sandwichs

Jeannot Lapin, the dormice—
Pierrot and Jacquot Loirs, Sophie,
Émile, Gustave, and Colbert
are enjoying a beautiful day for
a country picnic. The menu is
sandwiches plus berries and
hazelnuts they gather.

Makes 4 servings

Ingredients

Dough

About 1 1/2 cups all-purpose flour

1 package active dry yeast (regular or quick-rise)

1/2 teaspoon salt

1/2 teaspoon sugar

2/3 cup warm water, about body temperature

About 2 tablespoons olive oil

Sauce

1 can (6 oz.) tomato paste

1/2 cup prepared spaghetti (or marinara) sauce

Toppings

(Up to 1 cup total per pizza)

Thin sliced onions, mushrooms, red bell peppers, tomatoes, olives

Cooked crumbled Italian sausage

Chopped cooked chicken or ham

Basil leaves, rinsed and drained

Plus

Shredded mozzarella cheese (1 to 2 cups total)

Grated Parmesan cheese (about 1/2 cup total)

Tools

Bowls and fork or food processor

Flexible scraper

Plastic wrap

Paring knife

Rolling pin

2 baking sheets, 12 by 15 to 17 inches

Cutting board

Wide spatula

Crisp Pizza

Pizza Croustillante

Sophie,

You can buy dough at the supermarket, but it's more fun to make your own. It rises while you get the toppings ready.

Cleo and Henry

Dough

1. In a bowl or food processor, mix 1 1/2 cups flour, yeast, salt, and sugar. Add water and 1 tablespoon olive oil. Stir with a fork until ingredients hold together in a ball, or whirl in processor until dough lumps into a soft ball. Dough is soft and sticky. If using a food processor, leave dough in it, covered. If you mixed dough with a fork, scrape dough onto a counter coated with flour, and lightly dust dough with more flour. Also dust your hands with flour and knead dough (page 9) gently—take care not to tear dough surface—until it feels smooth and velvety, about 5 minutes. Put dough back in bowl; cover with plastic wrap. Let dough stand until very puffy, 1 to 1 1/2 hours.

2. If puffed dough is in the processor, whirl for a few seconds to beat out the air bubbles. Add 2 tablespoons flour; whirl, then scrape dough onto the floured counter. If dough is in the bowl, rub your hands with a little oil, punch dough down to get rid of the air, then scrape the dough onto the floured counter. Knead dough (page 9) several turns to make a smooth ball.

3. Cut dough ball into quarters. Knead each quarter on floured counter to make a smooth ball, adding flour to board as required to prevent sticking. BE CAREFUL not to break into or tear dough surface or it will get very sticky and pick up a lot more flour.

4. Working with 1 piece of dough at a time, pat it into a flat disk about 4 inches wide on floured counter. With a flour-dusted rolling pin, roll dough to make an 8-inch-wide round.

5. Rub baking sheets with oil. As each dough round is shaped, lift gently and set on pan, allowing room for 2 pieces per pan. Gently pull and stretch dough to make neatly shaped rounds. Dip your fingertips in olive oil and rub over dough to coat evenly.

6. Bake dough in a 400° oven until it is lightly browned, about 10 minutes (thin spots will be darker). Remove from oven; leave baked pizza crusts on pans at least 10 minutes or until cool.

Sauce

Scrape tomato paste into a bowl; add spaghetti sauce and mix. Spoon an equal amount of sauce onto each pizza crust, then spread sauce to rim.

Toppings/Plus

Scatter toppings in an even layer onto sauce on each pizza crust. Lay basil leaves over toppings. Sprinkle each pizza with about 1/4 of the mozzarella and Parmesan cheeses.

Bake in a 400° oven. After 5 minutes, move pans, changing racks for even cooking. Continue to bake until toppings are hot and cheeses melted, 8 to 10 minutes. Slide onto plates with spatula.

From: sophiesouris@jegrignote.fr

Makes 4 servings

Ingredients

4 round crusty rolls (each about 4 in. wide)

2 garlic cloves, peeled** and pressed or minced

6 tablespoons extra-virgin olive oil

2 tablespoons balsamic vinegar

1 teaspoon anchovy paste (optional)

1 can (6 oz.) tuna packed in water, drained

1 can (2.25 oz.) sliced black ripe olives

4 to 8 thin red onion and tomato slices (3 to 4 in. wide)

8 to 12 thin cross-cut red bell pepper rings (3 to 4 in. wide)

Salt and pepper

1 cup basil leaves, rinsed and drained

Tools

Serrated knife

Garlic press

Bowl

Fork

Spoon

Cutting board

Plastic wrap

Soaked Sandwich

Pan Bagnat

Dear Californians,

Here's a cool sandwich from the South of France. You can take it to the beach by your house and have it for lunch. The bread is soaked with a good dressing and filled with yummy foods. Have a good day.

Sophie

1. With the serrated knife, cut the rolls in half horizontally.

2. Pull out enough bread from bottoms and tops of rolls to make shallow hollows to hold the ingredients; save crumbs for other uses or the birds.

3. In a small bowl, combine garlic, olive oil, vinegar, and anchovy paste. Stir with a fork to mix well.

4. Turn roll pieces cut side up and evenly drizzle oil mixture from a spoon over the bread.

5. Onto the bottoms of rolls, spoon equal portions of tuna, breaking it into flakes to cover the bread. Cover equally with olives, onions, tomatoes, and red peppers. Sprinkle with salt and pepper, then cover with basil leaves.

6. Set tops on rolls and press each sandwich down firmly with your hands to compress and flatten slightly. You can eat now, or wrap snugly in plastic wrap and let mellow 1 to 2 hours for flavors to settle in, maybe while you carry sandwiches to a picnic.

**Technique

Lay the flat side of a wide knife blade on garlic clove on a counter and carefully hit with your fist to break garlic skin and make clove easy to peel.

From: cleo.henryraccoons@greenhill.com

Makes 1

Ingredients

2 slices bread (the kind you like)

Butter

Enough Cheddar, American, or Swiss cheese slices to cover a bread slice

Cooked broccoli buds (florets), about 3 pieces for a sandwich

Tools

Narrow spatula

Paring knife

Frying pan, with lid, that is just a little wider than 1 bread slice (or wide enough for 2 slices if you want to make 2 sandwiches at a time)

Wide spatula

Toasted Cheese Sandwich

Croque-Monsieur

Dear Sophie,

Our Mom cooks extra broccoli at dinner so we can have some for our sandwiches. I invented this combination because we love broccoli cheese soup and warm melty cheese with toast. Jeremy Duck prefers fresh snails. They're escargots, so he might be a French duck.

Henry and Cleo

1. Generously butter 2 slices of bread.

2. Lay 1 slice of the bread, buttered side down, in a frying pan.

3. Cover the bread in the pan with sliced cheese. If you add broccoli, blot buds with towels to dry, then cut buds in half lengthwise so they are flat on 1 side. Lay broccoli on cheese. Cover with the other bread slice, buttered side up.

4. Put a lid on the frying pan and set pan on medium heat. Cook until the bread is toasted on the bottom, 3 to 4 minutes (lift edge with spatula to peek). Turn sandwich over with wide spatula, cover pan again, and cook until sandwich bottom is toasted, 3 to 4 more minutes. Lift sandwich from pan with wide spatula and put on a plate. You can cut sandwich into halves or quarters.

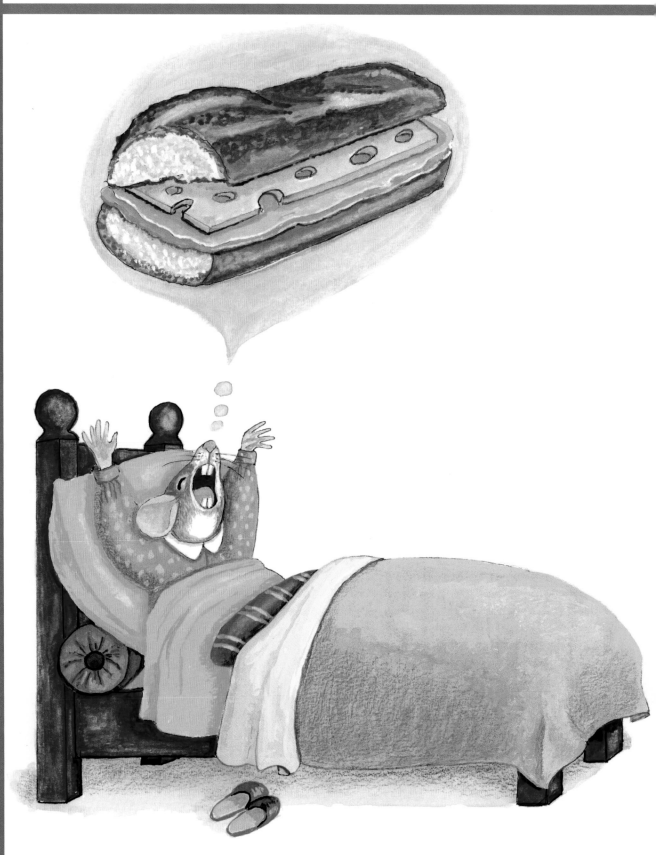

Lazy Sandwich

Sandwich Paresseux

Hey kids,

One more sandwich, so dreamy … as easy as un, deux, trois. Buttered baguette, good ham, Gruyère cheese. You can add lettuce, if you like. For Sunday outings, this is our favorite. Also take along some little sour French pickles—cornichons.

Sophie et famille

Makes 4 servings

Ingredients

1 very fresh long skinny baguette (1/2 lb.)

About 1/2 cup mayonnaise

About 1 1/2 tablespoons Dijon mustard

2 tablespoons chopped chives or green onions

About 1/2 pound thin-sliced cooked ham or roast beef

About 1/4 pound thin-sliced Gruyère or Swiss cheese

Tools

Serrated knife

Narrow spatula

1. With the serrated knife, horizonally cut the baguette in half lengthwise.

2. Spread cut sides of bread with mayonnaise, then the mustard. Sprinkle evenly with chives.

3. Overlap meat and cheese evenly on the bottom half of the baguette. Cover with the baguette top; cut sandwich crosswise into 4 equal pieces.

Cal Bear is a great cook. Red Fox, Henry, and Cleo are happy to be invited to dinner.

Main Dishes
Plats Principaux

From: sophiesouris@jegrignote.fr

Makes 6 to 8 servings

Ingredients

Press pastry (recipe at right)

All-purpose flour

1 cup finely chopped shallots or onion

2 tablespoons butter

4 large eggs

1 1/2 cups whipping cream or half-and-half cream

1 cup shredded Swiss cheese

1/4 teaspoon salt

1/4 teaspoon pepper

1/2 pound sliced cooked ham, coarsely chopped

Tools

9-inch quiche pan (with removable rim) or 9-inch pie pan at least 1 1/4 inches deep

Cutting board

French knife

Frying pan, 10 to 12 inches wide

Cooking spoon

Bowl

Fork

Pedestal, such as a can of broth

Pie server

Bonjour les copains,

My quiche is delish. It's easier to make than it looks. The boys really like it, too, but I think it's because they get to break the eggs.

Sophie

Quiche

Quiche

Press pastry

In a bowl or food processor, combine 1 1/2 cups all-purpose flour and 10 tablespoons (1/4 lb. plus 2 tablespoons) butter. Rub with your fingers, or whirl, until very fine crumbs. Add 1 large egg. Stir with a fork, or whirl, until dough forms a ball. Pat into a smooth 5- to 6-inch wide disk.

1. Put press pastry in quiche pan. Dust your hands with flour; using your fingers and palms, press pastry evenly over bottom and up the side of pan to make rim at least 1 1/4 inches high.

2. Put shallots and butter in frying pan. Stir often on medium-high heat until shallots are pale and limp, about 8 minutes. Pour into mixing bowl. Let cool at least 5 minutes.

3. Add eggs to bowl and beat with a fork to blend yolks and whites. Add cream, cheese, salt, and pepper; stir to blend.

4. Scatter ham over bottom of pastry-lined pan.

5. Set pan on center rack of a 375° oven (pull rack partially out, using hot pads), then carefully pour quiche filling into pan. Gently push rack into oven.

6. Bake quiche until pastry is golden brown and the filling puffs up, 40 to 45 minutes. Remove from oven and let quiche cool at least 10 minutes. Serve hot, warm, or at room temperature.

7. To remove pan rim, set pan on a pedestal of an upright can of food. Gently pull down rim and put quiche on a plate. Cut quiche in wedges and lift out portions with pie server.

Boiled Shrimp/Crevettes Cuites à l'Eau

Makes about 2 cups; 3 or 4 servings

Ingredients

Shrimp

1 pound (31 to 40 total) deveined raw shrimp in shells (buy with shells slit for easy peeling), thawed or frozen

3 quarts water

2 or 3 slices fresh ginger, each about the size of a quarter

Sauces

Nothing

Cocktail sauce

Catsup

Mustard

Mayonnaise

Lemon or lime juice

Tools

Pan, 4 to 5 quarts, with lid

Colander

Hey Sophie,

I dive for my dinner! Shrimp are good swimmers and they hide well. But I'm a good swimmer, too. Henry and I like shrimp plain—boiled, but very gently. You have to do it right or they get tough.

Cleo

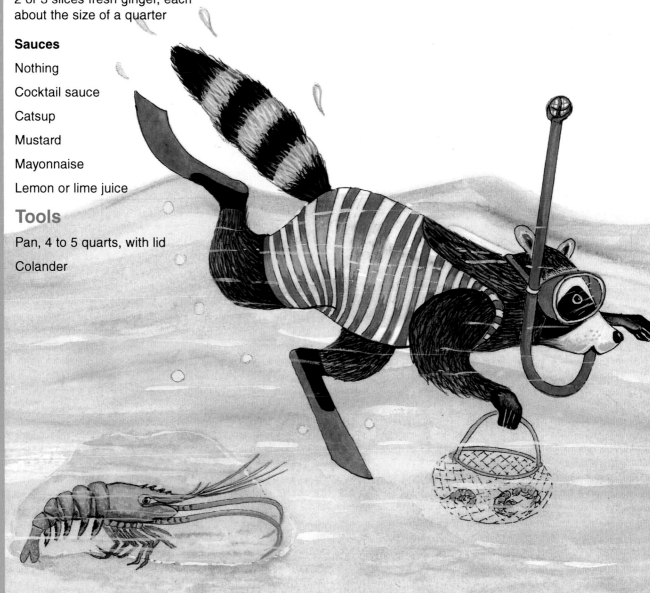

Boiled Shrimp

Crevettes Cuites à l'Eau

1. Put shrimp in colander and rinse well with cold running water.

2. Put 3 quarts water in pan, add ginger, and set on high heat until boiling, about 10 minutes.

3. Gently pour shrimp into water and put lid on pan. If shrimp are not frozen, take off heat and let stand 10 minutes. If shrimp are frozen, let water return to simmer, about 8 minutes, put lid on pan, remove pan from heat and let stand 5 minutes.

4. Using hot pads, pour shrimp into colander in the sink.

5. Peel shrimp** before serving, or as you eat them hot, warm, or cool. Eat plain, dipped into the sauce you like, or sprinkled with lemon or lime juice.

**Technique

To peel shrimp, you pull off the shell. But if you leave the last shell section on the tail, it makes a handle when you pick up the shrimp to eat it. Of course, the meat in the tail is good to eat, too.

Spring Lamb Stew/Navarin Printanier

Makes 4 servings

Ingredients

1 onion (1/2 lb.)

2 pounds boned, fat-trimmed lamb shoulder, cut into 1- or 2-inch chunks

3 cups chicken broth

2 Roma tomatoes (about 1/2 lb. total), rinsed

3 garlic cloves, peeled

1 bay leaf, fresh or dried

1 teaspoon dried thyme

2 carrots (1/4 lb. each), peeled

2 turnips (about 1/2 lb. total), peeled

8 thin-skin potatoes (about 1 1/4 in. wide), scrubbed, or 2 cups 1-inch cubes peeled potatoes

2 tablespoons cornstarch mixed with 1/4 cup water

1 cup frozen petite peas

1/2 cup chopped parsley

Salt and pepper

Tools

French knife

Cutting board

Pan, 5 to 6 quart, with lid

Cooking spoon

Timer

Vegetable peeler

Scrub brush

Good morning Cleo,

It's late afternoon here in Paris and I'm making lamb stew for tonight. We used to get lamb only in the spring, so that's why the stew has this name. It looks complicated because there are a lot of ingredients, but the steps are simple. Gustave is impatient for me to start. Goodbye.

Sophie

Spring Lamb Stew

Navarin Printanier

1. Peel onion, chop, and put in the pan.

2. Rinse lamb with cool water, drain, and put meat in the pan. Add 1/2 cup broth. Cover pan and set on high heat; when broth boils, reduce heat to simmer, and cook for 15 minutes. Uncover pan, turn heat to high, and stir occasionally with cooking spoon (use hot pad to hold handle) until all the liquid evaporates and dark brown stuff is stuck to pan, about 20 minutes. Pour another 1/2 cup broth into pan and stir to scrape the browned stuff free from pan. Pour remaining 2 cups broth into pan.

3. Cut out and discard stem ends of tomatoes. Cut tomatoes into big chunks and add, with their juices, to pan.

4. Chop garlic and add to pan with bay leaf and thyme. When the liquid in pan is boiling, reduce heat to simmer and put lid on pan. Set timer for 30 minutes.

5. While meat simmers, peel carrots and turnips. Cut carrots into about 1/2-inch-thick slices; cut turnips in 1/2-inch cubes. Also scrub whole potatoes.

6. When meat has cooked 30 minutes, add carrots, turnips, and potatoes to pan and stir. Cover and continue simmering until meat and potatoes are tender when pierced (stick with knife tip or fork), about 30 minutes; stir several times.

7. Stir cornstarch mixture into lamb stew, then add peas and chopped parsley. Stir until boiling. Taste, and add salt and pepper to season as you like. (If you want a thinner sauce, stir in a little more broth.) Ladle stew onto plates or into wide soup bowls.

Makes 4 or 5 servings

Ingredients

1 chicken (3 1/2 to 4 lb.)

2 tablespoons olive oil

4 or 5 thin-skin potatoes (1 1/2 to 2 in. wide), scrubbed

3 cups peeled baby carrots (about 1 lb.)

1 teaspoon dried thyme

About 3/4 teaspoon salt

1 lemon, rinsed, thinly sliced, and seeded

Pepper

Tools

Shallow rimmed pan, 10 by 15 inches

V-shape rack

Scrub brush

Vegetable peeler

Paring knife

Cooking spoon

2 forks

Bowl

Platter

Kitchen or poultry scissors or carving knife and fork

Sophie,

Stellar Jay tries to peck bites from the platter when I skate roast chicken with carrots and potatoes to the table. Such manners!! He's very crafty—and fast.

Henry

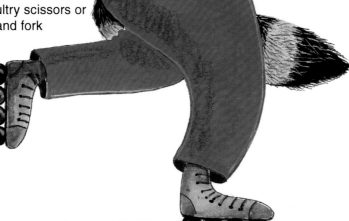

Roasted Chicken, Carrots, and Potatoes

Poulet Rôti, Carottes et Pommes de Terre

1. Rinse chicken inside and out with cold water; rinse giblets.

2. Rub rimmed pan with olive oil. Roll potatoes and carrots in oil; push to pan corner. Set V-shape rack, with sides tilted up, in pan. Set chicken, breast up, in rack. Put liver inside chicken; put the rest of giblets in pan.

3. Arrange potatoes and carrots around edge of rack; also put a layer of carrots under the chicken. Sprinkle thyme and 3/4 teaspoon salt evenly over chicken and vegetables. Put half the lemon slices inside chicken. Lay remaining slices on top chicken.

4. Roast in a 375° oven until chicken is browned, carrots are tinged with brown, and potatoes are soft when pressed (use hot pads), 1 hour to 1 hour and 15 minutes; stir vegetables several times.

5. With hot pads, set pan on a heatproof counter. Stick a fork into each side of chicken close to wing-breast joints. Tilt chicken to drain juices from body into pan. Then put chicken on a big platter. Stir vegetables with pan juices, then spoon vegetables around chicken. Pour juices in pan into a small bowl.

6. Cut chicken (scissors work great) into pieces. Snip or cut off wings at the wing-breast joints, drumsticks at drumstick-thigh joints, thighs at the thigh-body joints. Cut through the center of the breast and along bottom sides of ribs. Cut the back in half in the middle across backbone. Serve with vegetables and juice; add salt and pepper to taste.

Sometimes we use watercress to garnish the chicken platter. You can serve lemon wedges to squeeze onto the food to suit your taste.

From: sophiesouris@jegrignote.fr

Makes 4 servings

Ingredients

2 onions (1/2 lb. each)

2 garlic cloves

2 tablespoons butter

8 boned and skinned chicken thighs (about 1 3/4 lb. total)

2 cups chicken broth

1 bay leaf, fresh or dried

3/4 teaspoon dried thyme

1/2 teaspoon ground nutmeg

2 carrots (1/4 lb. each)

1/2 pound sliced mushrooms

1/4 cup all-purpose flour

1/4 cup water

1/2 cup whipping cream

1 1/2 tablespoons lemon juice

2 tablespoons chopped parsley

4 cups hot cooked rice

Salt and pepper

Tools

French knife

Cutting board

Pan, 4 to 5 quarts, with lid

Cooking spoon

Vegetable peeler

Fork

Bowl

Whisk

Dear Henry and Cleo,

We made your roast chicken and gobbled it up. See how you like our blanquette de poulet—it's simmered, not roasted. Be prepared to cry, though! Onion has an attitude. But it goes so well with creamy chicken.

Sophie

Creamy Chicken Stew

Blanquette de Poulet

1. Peel and chop onions and garlic. Put them with butter into the pan.

2. Set pan on medium-high heat and stir often until onions and garlic are limp, 10 to 12 minutes.

3. Rinse chicken thighs with cool water; cut off and discard any fat lumps. Put chicken in pan with broth, bay leaf, thyme, and nutmeg; cover with lid and turn heat to medium.

4. Rinse carrots, peel, and cut into 1-inch chunks. Add carrots and mushrooms to chicken. Turn heat to high; when boiling, reduce heat to simmer.

5. Simmer until chicken is tender enough to pull apart when prodded with a fork, about 40 minutes.

6. In a small bowl, combine the flour and water; whisk until smooth. Stir flour mixture and cream into the pan; turn heat to high and stir until sauce is rapidly boiling. Stir in lemon juice and parsley; remove pan from heat.

7. Spoon hot rice into wide bowls and ladle chicken and sauce over it. Add salt and pepper to taste.

From: cleo.henryraccoons@greenhill.com

Makes 4 servings

Ingredients

About 1 pound Italian turkey sausages (4 or 5)

3/4 cup milk

3/4 cup all-purpose flour

3 large eggs

1/4 teaspoon salt

Tools

Paring knife

Baking pan, oval 7 by 12 inches or 8 inches square (6 to 7 cups)

Blender

Flexible scraper

Sophie,

Mr. Toad, a grumpy old neighbor, doesn't like the name of this dish. He says, "Why am I accused of hiding in a hole? It's more comfy under a big boletus mushroom." If he'd just come and eat Toad in a Hole with us some weekend morning or for supper, he'd change his mind and even smile!

Cleo

Toad in a Hole

Crapaud dans un Trou

1. Cut sausages in half crosswise and lay pieces side by side in the pan.

2. Bake in a 375° oven until sausages are lightly browned and juicy, 20 to 25 minutes.

3. While sausages bake, put milk, flour, eggs, and salt in a blender; cover and whirl until flour is totally blended with liquid (no lumps).

4. Open oven, pull rack (use hot pads) with sausage pan out far enough to pour milk mixture around sausages.

5. Push rack back into oven. Bake until egg pudding mixture puffs high and is really browned, 40 to 45 minutes.

6. With hot pads, take pan to table and set on another hot pad. With a big spoon, scoop pudding and sausages onto plates.

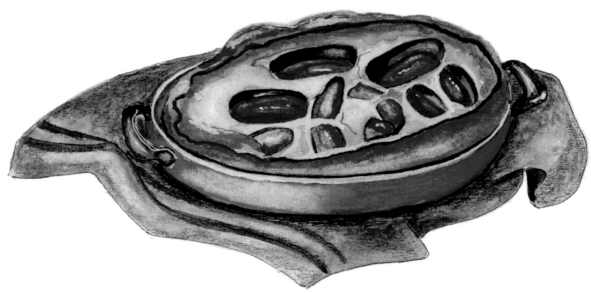

Spicy Pork Ribs/Échine de Porc Épicée

Makes 2 or 3 grown-up servings

Ingredients

1 slab pork back ribs (about 2 lb. with 12 to 14 bones, whole or in several pieces)

2 teaspoons paprika

1 teaspoon rubbed dried sage

1/2 teaspoon ground cumin

1/2 teaspoon salt

1/2 teaspoon pepper

Tools

Paper towels

Shallow rimmed pan, 10 by 15 inches or 12 by 17 inches

Bowl

Fork

Kitchen scissors

Spicy Pork Ribs

Échine de Porc Épicée

Howdy Sophie,

Our West isn't very wild anymore and you don't need to be a cowboy to rope in great tasting ribs. Just pop 'em in the oven and roast nice and juicy.

Henry

1. Rinse pork ribs with cool water, then pat dry with paper towels. Lay ribs in rimmed pan.

2. In a small bowl, stir together the paprika, sage, cumin, salt, and pepper. Rub all the spice mixture over the pork ribs.

3. Lay ribs meaty side up in a single layer in pan.

4. Put ribs in a 375° oven and bake until meat is well browned and begins to shrink back from the ends of the bones, 1 hour to 1 hour and 15 minutes.

5. With hot pads, take pan from oven and set on a heatproof counter. Brace ribs with fork and use scissors to cut between every 2 or 3 bones to separate pieces. Pile ribs on a platter. Eat hot.

Tip
It's easy to increase this recipe to make 4 to 6 servings. Just use 2 slabs of ribs and double the amount of seasonings. All these ribs will fit in a 12- by 17-inch pan.

Desserts

Desserts

Fruits make perfect desserts—naturally. They're also awesome used in desserts. Chocolate, crêpes, and cake are fab, too!

From: sophiesouris@jegrignote.fr

Makes 5 or 6 servings

Ingredients

8 ounces (1/2 lb.) semisweet or bittersweet chocolate, chips or chopped

1 tablespoon milk

1 tablespoon butter

4 large egg whites (or 1/2 cup pasteurized egg whites that can be whipped)

1/4 teaspoon salt

1/3 cup sugar

Tools

Glass bowl

Microwave oven

Flexible scraper

Bowl

Electric mixer

Dessert bowls

Plastic wrap

Chocolate Mousse

Mousse au Chocolat

Bonjour les amis,

Uncle Yo says, "Chocolate mousse is perfect if it stays in the bowl when you turn it upside down." Leon dared Azie to try, but I warned, "Don't do it in your party dress. A mouse under a mousse might get messy."

Sophie

1. Put chocolate, milk, and butter in a glass bowl. Heat in the microwave oven on high (full power) for 30 seconds. Stir chocolate with a flexible scraper. Heat 15 seconds more; stir again and if there are still lumps of chocolate, heat 15 seconds and stir again until smooth. Let stand at least 5 minutes to cool.

2. Put egg whites and salt in a large deep bowl. Beat with mixer on high speed until whites are foamy, then add sugar, 1 tablespoon at a time, continuing to beat until whites hold sharp peaks. To test, turn off mixer and lift up beater; the whites should make stiff peaks.

3. Scoop about 1/3 of the whites into the melted chocolate; stir with scraper to mix well. Scrape remaining whites into chocolate mixture and fold gently with scraper until there are no white streaks, but don't stir; you want to keep the mixture fluffy.

4. Scrape chocolate mousse into a serving bowl or into individual bowls. Cover airtight with plastic wrap and chill until firm, at least 6 hours or up to 2 days.

Tip
For an even more velvety mousse, stir 1 or 2 of the egg yolks into the melted chocolate.

From: cleo.henryraccoons@greenhill.com

Makes 2 servings

Ingredients

1 firm-ripe to ripe mango (any kind, 8 to 12 oz.) or 1 to 1 1/2 cups frozen mango chunks

1 ripe banana (6 to 7 in. long)

1 carton (6 oz.) or 3/4 cup plain or fruit flavor yogurt

1/2 to 3/4 cup orange juice or tangerine juice

Ice cubes (optional)

Tools

Paring knife

Blender or food processor

Flexible scraper

Tall glasses

Drinking straws

Mango Smoothie

Velouté de Mangue

To Sophie and the gang,

Smooth, cool, super easy. For dessert, breakfast, or a snack, smoothies are sweet tum-yums. Cheers.

Cleo

1. With paring knife, cut off mango skin and discard.

2. Cut fruit off mango pit and put in blender (food processor works but mixture won't be as smooth). Discard pit (first, bite off fruit scraps). Or use frozen mango chunks.

3. Peel banana and break into chunks into the blender or processor. Scrape yogurt in with fruit. Add orange juice. If fruit is room temperature, add 2 or 3 ice cubes. Cover and whirl until mixture is very smooth. Pour into tall glasses and sip through straws.

From: sophiesouris@jegrignote.fr

Makes 15 or 16; 4 or 5 servings

Ingredients

Batter

1 cup milk
4 1/2 teaspoons melted butter
3 large eggs
1/2 cup all-purpose flour

Fillings

(Your choice)
Sugar
Lemon or orange wedges
Grated chocolate
Jam
Butter
Nutella
Honey
Apple or pear butter

Tools

Blender or bowl and whisk
Flexible scraper
Crêpe pan or nonstick frying pan,
6 to 7 inches across bottom

Measuring cup or ladle
that holds 3 tablespoons
Wide spatula
Plate (microwave oven-safe)

Bonjour les Californiens,

When Uncle Yo comes for the holidays, he makes crêpes and we help. He taught us how to flip them in the air and even little Clara can do it! Merci for the smoothie recipe, Cleo; fresh mangos seem to be around all year.

Sophie

Tip

To make a double batch of crêpes, put twice the amount of each ingredient in the blender. If you don't want to cook the crêpes all at the same time, the batter keeps in the refrigerator 2 days; mix to use.

Crêpes or Thin Pancakes

Crêpes

1. Put milk, 4 teaspoons butter, and eggs in blender. Then add the flour. Cover blender, turn to high speed, and whirl until the crêpe batter is smoothly mixed; if flour sticks in the blender, stop motor, scrape flour free, cover again, and whirl some more. (Or put flour in a big bowl and add milk in 1/2-cup portions, whisking each addition until there are no lumps. Add eggs and 4 teaspoons butter and beat with whisk until batter is smooth.)

2. Set crêpe pan on medium-high heat. When the pan is hot enough to make a drop of water dance, put remaining 1/2 teaspoon butter in pan and tilt to coat the pan bottom. You won't need to do this again.

3. Add to pan all at once 3 tablespoons batter.

4. Quickly tilt pan so batter coats the bottom evenly to the edge; a few tiny bubbles and holes are no problem. Cook crêpe until the rim is brown and the surface is firm and dry, less than a minute.

5. Slide spatula around pan edge under the crêpe rim to make sure it isn't stuck, then slide the spatula all the way under the crêpe and quickly turn it over. Cook crêpe long enough to brown a little bit on the bottom, about 1/2 minute. Lift pan off the heat and quickly flip it over to drop crêpe onto a plate.

6. To make each remaining crêpe, follow steps 3, 4, and 5 and stack.

7. You can eat the crêpes as you make them; stacked they will be warm when all are cooked. If you want hot crêpes, put the stack on the plate in the microwave oven and heat on high (full power) until hot to touch, about 1 minute.

8. To flavor crêpes, sprinkle each with a little sugar and add a squeeze of lemon juice or orange juice; sprinkle with grated chocolate; or dot or spread with jam, butter, Nutella, honey, or fruit butter. To enclose the filling, fold or roll crêpe as the drawing above shows, and eat.

Blueberry Oatmeal Crumble/Croustade de Myrtilles aux Flocons d'Avoine

Makes 5 or 6 servings

Ingredients

Filling

3 cups blueberries, fresh or frozen

2 tablespoons packed brown sugar

1 tablespoon all-purpose flour

1 teaspoon grated lemon peel

1 tablespoon lemon juice

Crumble

3/4 cup rolled oats (5-minute kind)

1/4 cup all-purpose flour

1/4 cup packed brown sugar

3 tablespoons butter

Tools

Colander

Baking dish, about 6 by 10 inches,
1 1/2 inches deep (4 to 5 cups)

Cooking spoon

Bowl

Sophie,

Ralph Chipmunk, who lives next door, picks healthy foods, so for dessert he chooses blueberries—carefully sorting out the best ones—for a warm oatmeal crumble. He sings, "Blueberries preserve memory," off-tune. We think you'll like his dessert, even if it's good for you.

Henry and Cleo

78

Blueberry Oatmeal Crumble

Croustade de Myrtilles aux Flocons d'Avoine

Filling

1. Sort fresh berries, picking out and discarding soft ones. Put fresh berries in a colander and rinse well with cool running water; let drain.

2. In baking dish, mix the brown sugar, flour, and lemon peel. Add fresh or frozen berries and lemon juice; mix gently. Shake dish gently to make berries level.

Crumble

3. In a bowl, rub oats, flour, sugar, and butter with your fingers until lumps stick together. Scatter mixture over the berries and press gently to make a flat layer on fruit.

4. Put blueberry crumble in a 375° oven and bake until fruit mixture bubbles and topping is browned, about 50 minutes.

5. Scoop blueberry crumble, hot or warm, into dessert bowls.

This is really best eaten with vanilla ice cream.

From: sophiesouris@jegrignote.fr

Makes 8 servings

Ingredients

1 carton (6 oz., 3/4 cup) plain yogurt

2 yogurt cartons sugar

3 yogurt cartons all-purpose flour

2 large eggs

2 teaspoons baking powder

6 tablespoons melted butter

Grated peel of 1 orange or lemon

More butter and all-purpose flour

Tools

Flexible scraper

Food processor or bowl and whisk

Grater/shredder

Baking dish or pan, 7 by 11 inches, at least 1 1/2 inches deep

Yogurt Cake

Gâteau au Yaourt

Bonjour les copains,

Gustave painted the kitchen wall with the recipe for Clara's favorite cake. We think it looks nice, and it's certainly useful. Clara prefers her gâteau au yaourt warm with cream cheese and jam, especially after school.

Sophie

1. Scrape all the yogurt into food processor or bowl. Rinse and dry yogurt carton. Use carton to measure sugar and flour, filling it to the rim and scraping top level; add to yogurt. Then add eggs, baking powder, melted butter, and grated peel. Whirl or whisk until batter is very well mixed.

2. Butter the baking dish, add about 1 tablespoon flour, and tilt and shake dish to coat bottom and sides with flour. Dump and discard the extra flour. Scrape cake batter into the dish; spread level.

3. Bake cake on the center rack in a 325° oven until it is nicely browned, begins to pull from dish sides, and center, when lightly touched with your finger, pops back up, about 1 hour.

4. Take cake out of oven (use hot pads) and let stand on a heatproof counter at least 20 minutes; serve hot, warm, or cool, cut into rectangles.

From: cleo.henryraccoons@greenhill.com

Makes 6 to 8 servings

Ingredients

Crust

1 cup all-purpose flour

1/4 cup sugar

6 tablespoons butter, cut in chunks

1 large egg

Filling

2 Golden Delicious or Pink Lady apples (about 1 lb. total)

2 tablespoons sugar

1/4 teaspoon ground cinnamon

2 teaspoons butter, cut in little pieces

Topping

Whipped cream flavored with powdered sugar and vanilla, or vanilla ice cream

Tools

Food processor or bowl and fork

Baking sheet, 15 by 17 inches

Rolling pin

Vegetable peeler

Paring knife

Narrow spatulas

Plate

Hello Sophie and company,

Sly Coyote is the bandit who steals our apples every year. We have to guard the tree to have plenty of fruit for country apple tarts. The crust always stays tender and flaky no matter how much you squeeze or push it around.

Henry and Cleo

Country Apple Tart

Tarte Campagnarde aux Pommes

Crust

1. Put 1 cup flour, sugar, and butter in a food processor. Cover and whirl until mixture is crumbly. (Or put flour, sugar, and butter in a bowl; rub with your fingers until crumbly.)

2. Add egg; whirl or stir with a fork until dough holds together in a smooth lump.

3. Dust your hands with a little flour; firmly press dough into a smooth ball. Pat ball to make a disk 4 to 5 inches wide. Lay dough on baking sheet.

4. Rub your hands with more flour and, with the flat of your palm, press the dough to make an evenly thick round about 12 inches wide right up the pan edge. (Or roll dough with a floured rolling pin.)

Filling

5. Rinse apples, peel, cut into quarters, and cut out and discard core, stem, and peel. Cut each quarter into 3 or 4 slices.

6. Lay apple slices in an overlapping circle on dough, starting about 1 1/2 inches in from edge of dough round. Continue to lay slices in overlapping circles to the center. Then fit any leftover apples slices into the circle.

7. With your fingers (or short narrow spatula), lift up dough edge and lay it over onto apples. (If dough gets really soft, scrape it up against apples with spatula.)

8. With your hands, press dough against fruit to make a neat rim and give the tart a nice round shape.

9. Mix sugar and cinnamon; sprinkle evenly over fruit and pastry. Dot apples with little butter pieces.

10. Bake tart on the center rack in a 375° oven until pastry is a rich golden brown and apples are tender when you stick them with a knife tip, about 45 minutes.

11. Using hot pads, take pan from oven and set on a heatproof counter. Slide a long narrow spatula under tart to make sure it isn't stuck. Let stand 10 minutes or until cool. Tip pan and slide tart onto a plate. Cut tart into wedges and serve with whipped cream.

From: sophiesouris@jegrignote.fr

Makes 10; 5 to 10 servings

Ingredients

Éclairs

1/2 cup water

1/4 cup (1/8 lb.) butter, cut into chunks

2 teaspoons sugar

1/2 cup all-purpose flour

2 large eggs

Filling

1/4 cup sugar

1 tablespoon cornstarch

1/2 cup milk

1 teaspoon vanilla

1 large egg

1 tablespoon butter

(Or whipped cream from a squirt can, or 1 cup whipped cream sweetened to taste with sugar)

Frosting

1 cup semisweet chocolate chips

2 tablespoons milk

Tools

Pan, 1 1/2 to 2 quarts

Cooking spoon

Flexible scraper

Pastry bag with plain 3/4 inch opening or 2 spoons

Baking sheet, 12 by 15 inches

Cooling rack

Serrated knife

Narrow spatula

Whisk

2-cup glass measuring cup

Microwave oven

Éclairs
Éclairs

Henry and Cleo,

Éclairs are totally French and soooo good. You have to make them!!

Sophie

Éclairs

1. Put water, butter, and sugar in pan and set on high heat. When water is boiling, stir to melt butter.

2. Hold pan firmly with hot pad and dump flour into pan; stir vigorously with spoon until flour mixture has no lumps and comes together in a ball from the pan sides; this happens quickly.

3. Take pan off the heat and let stand 10 minutes. Make an impression in dough with cooking spoon. Break 1 egg into the hollow. Beat vigorously until batter is well mixed. Add remaining egg and beat to blend.

4. Use scraper to scoop all the dough into the pastry bag. Twist bag top snugly down against the dough.

5. Hold bag vertically, tip down with top held shut, and squeeze dough into 10 equal-size logs, each 4 inches long, and at least 1 inch apart on baking sheet. You may need to make more than 1 squeeze per log to come out even. To make neat logs, wet your hands in water, and lightly smooth dough with you fingers. (Or spoon dough in 10 equal portions onto baking sheet; shape logs with wet hands.)

6. Bake éclairs on center rack in a 400° oven until well browned and crisp, about 20 minutes.

7. With hot pads, remove baking sheet from oven and gently slide éclairs onto a cooling rack; if stuck, slide spatula under éclairs to release them. When cool enough to touch, carefully cut each éclair almost in half lengthwise from a long side with a serrated knife; don't detach top.

Filling

8. Rinse and dry pan used for éclairs. Add sugar and cornstarch, mix, then stir in milk, vanilla, and egg. Add butter.

9. Set pan on medium-high heat and stir with a whisk until mixture boils vigorously and is very thick. Remove from heat and let stand until lukewarm or cool; stir now and then to keep smooth.

Frosting

Put chocolate and milk in the glass measuring cup. Heat in microwave oven on high (full power) for 30 seconds. Stir with flexible scraper until chocolate is smooth.

Fill and frost éclairs

10. Gently lift top on each éclair and spoon vanilla filling equally into the hollows, using all (or fill éclairs with whipped cream); set tops back in place.

11. Stir frosting and spoon equal amounts onto each filled éclair, guiding frosting with back of spoon to cover tops. Set éclairs on a plate and chill about 10 minutes to firm frosting.

12. Eat, or cover airtight (without touching frosting). Keep cold. Serve éclairs within 4 hours for best texture; they soften on standing.

Makes 6 servings

Ingredients

2 to 3 tablespoons dried shredded sweetened coconut

1 cup whipping cream*

1/4 cup powdered sugar

1 teaspoon vanilla

14 flat macaroon cookies with coconut (each about 3 in. wide)

Tools

Frying pan, 8 to 10 inches

Cooking spoon

Bowls

Electric mixer

Plate, flat for at least 9-inches across inside rim

Narrow spatulas

Flexible scraper

Paper towels

French knife or sharp cake knife

Pie server

*Tip

Cream has to be cold to whip well. It also helps if the bowl and beaters are chilled.

Sophie,

There's no baking when you make this dessert. But the cake has to chill overnight for the cookies to soften so the cake cuts neatly. Thank you for the éclair recipe; no wonder you are famous for them.

Cleo

Coconut Cooky Cream Cake

Gâteau-Biscuit à la Noix de Coco et Crême

1. Put coconut in frying pan. Set on medium heat and stir often until coconut is lightly toasted, about 2 minutes. Pour into a little bowl.

2. Pour cream into a chilled deep bowl. With mixer on high speed, beat cream until it is thick enough to hold soft peaks (lift beater to see). Add powdered sugar and vanilla. Mix on slow speed to blend.

3. On flat plate, arrange 7 cookies, 6 in a circle with 1 in the middle, edges touching. With a short narrow spatula, put a little dab of cream on the bottom of each cooky and set back into the circle so it won't slide around.

4. Spoon about half of the whipped cream onto the center of the cookies. With a long narrow spatula, spread cream level over cookies, following their curves to the outside edges.

5. Keeping the flower shape, set 7 cookies directly on top of the ones on the plate. With scraper, scoop the remaining cream onto cookies. Spread cream level to edges, then push over edges to frost sides; hold short spatula

vertically to evenly coat sides with cream. Use paper towels to wipe smears off the plate.

6. Scatter coconut onto the cake top. Invert a large bowl (big enough not to touch dessert) over cake and refrigerate until the next day so cookies will soften enough to cut without breaking.

7. Lift off bowl. With sharp knife, cut cake into 6 equal wedges. Lift out pieces with pie server. If you have cake left, cover with bowl and chill; it's good for 2 more days.

Glossary Pronunciation Guide

Just like English, French has its own special set of sounds! Sometimes it can be hard to pronounce a new language because of all the new sounds that we don't know how to say. There are some sounds in French that we don't even use in English at all! You can use the tips below to help you pronounce the words in the glossary.

*   ü – This sounds kind of like our *u* sound, only it's even longer. You can make the *ü* sound by making a long *eeeeeee* and rounding your lips at the same time. You use it in French words like *une.*

*   zh – This is a sound that we do have in English. It's kind of like the *j* sound, only a little bit shorter. We use it in words like: *treasure* and *measure.* You use it in French words like *j'aime.*

*   õ – This is like an *o* sound with more air coming out of the nose. Try making it by pretending that you're going to say *om* without actually saying the *m* at the end. You use it in French words like *bonjour!*

*   ã – Just like the *õ,* this sound is made with more air coming out of your nose. Try making it by saying *haunt* without the *nt* at the end. You use it in French words like *blanc.*

*   ĩ – This is another nose sound. Try making it by saying *ant,* without the *nt* at the end. You use it in French words like *pain* and *bain.*

*   One last note about the glossary pronunciation:
    ah: Pronounce as in *ah ha!*
    ih: Pronounce as the *i* in *bit* or *sit.*
    eh: Pronounce as the *e* in *bed* or *said.*
    uh: Pronounce as the *u* in *bud* or *sud.*
    oh: Pronounce as the *o* in *boat* or *wrote.*

Julie Olsen

French en français	How to say Comment dire	English en anglais
à	ah	to; in other contexts at, in, into, on, by, for, from, with
ail	ahyee	garlic
amis	ah-mee	friends
anglais	ã-gleh	English
appétit	ah-pet-ee	appetite
artichauts	are-tee-sho	artichokes
attention	ah-tens-yõ	caution
au, aux	oh	to the; contraction of à le, à les
avec	ah-veck	with
Azie	ah-zee	feminine nickname
bagnat	bang-yah	bathed; Provençal word
baguette	bah-get	long skinny bread loaf
base	bahz	base
batteur	bah-ter	mixer, beater
beurre	beur	butter
bien	bee-yĩ	good, well
biscuits	bee-ss-kwee	cookies
blanquette	blã-ket	ragoût or stew with white sauce
bois	bwah	wood, woods
boite	bwat	box
bols	buhl	bowls
bon, bons	bõ	good, kind
bon appétit	bun a-pet-ee	good appetite
bonjour	bõ-zhoor	good day
Bois de Boulogne	bwah duh boo-lunga	a big park in Paris
cacahuète	ah -kah-wet	peanut
Californiens	ka-lee-for-nee-yĩ	Californians
campagnarde	kã -pang-yard	rustic, rural, from the countryside
carottes	kar -uh-t	carrots
casseroles	kass-er-uhl	cooking pans
César	sih-zar	Caesar
c'est	sih	it is
c'est bien vrai	sih byĩ vreh	it's so true
chaudrée	sho-drih	from chaudronnée, a hot fish soup named for the cooking container, chaudron

French	How to say	English
chaudron	sho-drõ	a cooking container
chaudronnée	sho-dro-nih	a hot fish soup
chocolat	sho-ko-lah	chocolate
ciseaux	see-zoh	scissors
citron	see-trõ	lemon
cochon	koh-shõ	pig
Colbert	kol-bair	Colbert
comment dire	kom-ã deer	how to say
copains	koh-pĩ	chums, pals
cornichons	kor-nee-shõ	small sour pickles
courgettes	koor-zhet	zucchini, summer squash
couteau, couteaux	koo-toh	knife, knives
couteau-scie	koo-toh see	serrated knife
couvercles	koo-vair-kluh	lids
crapaud	krah-poh	toad
crême	kr-eh-m	cream
crêpe	kr-eh-p	thin pancakes
crevettes	kr-uh-vet	shrimp
croque	kr-uh-k	crackles between the teeth
croque-monsieur	kr-uh-k muss-yuh	grilled cheese and ham sandwich
croquer	kr-uh-kih	to crackle between the teeth
croustade	kroos-tad	dish prepared with crust
croustillante	kroos-tee-yã	crisp, crusty
crudités	krew-dee-tih	small pieces of raw vegetables
cuillère, cuillères	kwee-yair	spoon, spoons
cuisine	kwee-zeen	cooking, kitchen
cuites	kweet	cooked
d'avoine	dav-wan	of oats, contraction of de avoine
d'aluminium	dal-üm-een-yum	
papier	pah-p-yih	foil, paper of aluminum
dans	dã	in
de	duh	of
découper	dih-koo-pih	to cut up (vegetables) or to carve (a piece of meat)
desserts	dih-sair	desserts
deux	duh	two
d'oeuvre	duh-vre	of works, d', contraction of de
échine	ih-sheen	backbone.
éclairs	ih-klair	éclairs
électrique	eh-leck-treek	electric
elle	el	she

French	How to say	English
Émile	Eih-meel	Emil
en (dans)	ã (on)	in
épicée	ih-pee-ss	spicy
éplucheur	ih-plew-sher	peeler
escargot	iss-kar-go	snail
et	ih	and
faire	fair	to do
famille	fam-eey	family
farcies	far-see	stuffed
fermière	fair-mee-yair	from the farm, farm woman
fine	feen	fine
flocons	flok-ō	flakes
forme	form	shape
fouet	fweh	whisk
four	foor	oven
fourchette	foor-shet	fork
fraîches	fresh	fresh
français	frã-she	French
frire	freer	to fry
gants	gã	gloves
gaspacho	gass-patch-oh	gazpacho
gâteau	gah-toh	cake
gâteau-biscuits	gah-toh bee-ss-kwee	cooky cake
Géraldine	zhair-al-deen	Geraldine
gougères	goo-zhair	cheese cream puffs
grattoir	grah-twar	scraper
grenouille	gruh-nooy	frog
grignote	green-yut	gnaw, nibble
grille	greey	grill
Gruyère	groo-yair	a kind of cheese
Gustave	güst-av	Gustave
haricots	ah-ree-koh	beans
haricots verts	ah-ree-koh vair	green beans
hors	or	out of, outside
hors-d'oeuvre	or dove-ruh	appetizers
il	eel	he
Jacquot	zhack-oh	Jack
je	zhuh	I
Jeannot	zhan-oh	Johnny

French	How to say	English
jegrignote.fr	zhuh-green-yut pwĩ eff air	Sophie's e-mail address, fr is for France
Jules	Julzhül	Jules
La Vache Qui Rit	lah vash kee ree	the laughing cow, a brand of cheese
le, la	luh, lah	the; le is masculine, la is feminine
l'eau	loh	the water; l', contraction of la before a vowel
légumes	lih-güm	vegetables
Léon	lih-yõ	Leon
les	lih	the; neutral gender when plural
loirs	luh-w-ar	dormice
Louvre	loo-vruh	a museum in Paris
macédoine	mah-sih-dwan	mixed vegetables
mangue	mã-guh	mango
merci	mair-see	thank you
mesurer	muh-zü-rih	to measure
micro-ondes	mee-kroh-onde	microwave
minces	mĩss	narrow
minuterie	meen-ü-tree	timer
mixer	meek-sih	blender, mixer, beater
monsieur	muss-yuh	sir, mister
moule	mool	mold
mousse	moo-ss	mousse
myrtilles	meer-teey	blueberries
navarin	nah-vah-rĩ	lamb or mutton stew with turnips and potatoes
noix	nwah	walnut
noix de coco	nwah duh koh-koh	coconut
ondes	õd	waves
ou	oo	or
ouvre	oov-ruh	open
ouvre-boîte	oov-ruh bwat	can opener
pan	pã	bread; Provençal word
pain	pĩ	bread
papier	pap-yih	paper
paresseux	pah-rih-suh	lazy
passoire	pass-w-ar	strainer, colander
pâtisserie	pah-tee-suh-ree	pastry
Pierrot	pee-yair-oh	Pete
pinceau	pĩ-soh	paint brush
pipelette	peep-let	slang for a talkative person a babbler, a chatterer

French	How to say	English
pique-niques	peek-neek	picnics
planche	plãsh	plank, board
plaques	plack-et	slabs for baking, baking sheets
plats	plah	serving dishes, finished food dishes
poche	puh-sh	pocket
poche à douille	puh-sh ah dooy	pastry bag
poêle, poêles	pwahl	frying pan, frying pans
pommes	puhm	apples
pommes de terre	puhm duh-tair	potatoes, earth apples
porc	por	pork
potiron	poh-tee-rõ	pumpkin
poulet	poo-leh	chicken
praires	prair	clams
presse	preh-ss	press
presse-citron	preh-ss see-trõ	lemon juicer
presse-ail	preh-ss ayee	garlic press
presse-purée	pr-eh-ss pü-rih	potato-masher
principaux	prĩ-see-poh	principal, most important
printanier	prĩ-tan-yih	springlike
Provençal	pro-vã-sal	language of Provence
Provence	pro-vãs	a region in southern France with its own language
purée	pü-rih	mashed potatoes
queue	kuh	tail
qui	kee	who
quiche	keesh	pie with savory custard filling
queue-de-cochon	kuh duh ko-shõ	pig's tail
ragoût	rah-goo	stew
râpe	rap	grater, shredder
récurer	rih-ku-rih	to scour, to cleanse
refroidir	ruh-fr-wah-deer	to cool
règles	regg-luh	rules
rémoulade	ruh-moo-lad	tangy sauce
rit (il rit, elle rit)	ree	he laughs, she laughs
rire	reer	to laugh
robot de cuisine	roh-boh duh kwee-zeen	food processor, kitchen robot
rôti	roh-tee	roast, roasted
rouleaux, rouleau	roo-loh	rolls, roll
salade, salades	sa-lad	salad, salads
salut	sa-lü	hello

French	How to say	English
sandwich, sandwichs	sand-weech	sandwich, sandwiches
sauce	sausoh-ss	sauce
savoir	sav-w-ar	to know
savoir-faire	sav-w-ar fair	how to, to know how to do
scie	see	saw
serviettes	sair-vee-yet	napkins
soupe, soupes	soop	soup, soups
souris	soo-ree	mouse, mice
spatules	spat-üle	spatulas
tarte	tart	pie
tartine	tart-een	bread slices
tasses	tass	cups
terre	tair	earth
tomates	tuh-mat	tomatoes
trois	trwah	three
trou	troo	hole
un	ĩn	one, masculine
une	ün	one, feminine
ustenciles	üs-tã-seel	tools
vache	vash	cow
velouté	vuh-loo-tih	velvetlike, soft and smooth
verts	vair	green (plural)
vrai	vreh	true, real
yaourt	yah-oor-t	yogurt

My Recipes

ISBN 142516855-8